Don't miss these other record-breaking books!

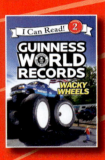

GUINNESS WORLD RECORDS

TOYS, GAMES, AND MORE!

by CHRISTA ROBERTS

HARPER

An Imprint of HarperCollinsPublishers

Library of Congress Control Number: 2016938975
ISBN 978-0-06-234172-3

Design by Victor Joseph Ochoa and Erica DeChavez
16 17 18 19 20   PC/RRDC   10 9 8 7 6 5 4 3 2 1
❖
First Edition

TABLE OF CONTENTS

INTRODUCTION

Anyone, anywhere, has the potential to be a record-breaker! For over 60 years, Guinness World Records (GWR) has timed, weighed, measured, verified, and documented thousands of the world's record-breakers in every category that you can imagine. There are over 40,000 current records!

Record-breaking is free to do. If the GWR adjudicators (the official judges who confirm records) approve your idea for a new record—or if you can prove you've bettered an existing title—you're on your way to becoming Officially Amazing!

Toys, Games, and More! is filled with playthings that are as fun as they are serious when it comes to breaking records. You'll find over 100 of them, from rubber duckies to building blocks, classic toys like yo-yos to the most popular arcade games, and none of these toys are playing around.

Take a look in your closet or dig around in your toy chest—you might just spot something that could help you earn a record of your own.

CHAPTER 1
Rubik's Cubes and Puzzles

Solving a Rubik's Cube is a big accomplishment in itself. But that impressive feat isn't enough for this cryptic-crazy crew. Read on for some amazing stories of puzzle prowess, from Rubik's Cubes to jigsaw puzzles to a devil's knot—and meet a robot that can beat any human in a Rubik's race, hands down!

ULTIMATE FACT:
There are 43,252,003,274,489,856,000 ways to scramble a Rubik's Cube!

FAST FINGERS

The Rubik's Cube is one of the most difficult puzzles to solve . . . unless you're **Eric Limeback**. The Canadian speed-cuber unscrambled 5,800 Rubik's Cubes in one day—the **most Rubik's Cubes solved in 24 hours**—at Wilfrid Laurier University in Waterloo, Ontario, Canada, on October 3, 2013. If you're wondering what a "speed-cuber" is, it's someone who solves twisty puzzles like the Rubik's Cube as quickly as possible!

PUZZLE POWER

The Rubik's Cube is one of the best-selling toys of all time—over 350 million have been bought worldwide since it launched, and people such as the team members of **Cubing Italy** are part of the reason why. These puzzle-lovers solved the **most Rubik's Cubes in one hour by a team**: 1,860. They achieved the record in Mantova, Italy, on October 16, 2010. Of the total, 260 were unscrambled by the leading team member, Max Iovane.

PUZZLERS AT WORK

The people that puzzle together, solve together at the **College of Engineering** in Pune, Maharashtra, India. On November 4, 2012, a total of 3,248 puzzlers came together to earn the title for **most people solving Rubik's Cubes simultaneously**.

A PUZZLE A DAY

You might say German **Sébastien Auroux** is a year-round fan of Rubik's Cubes—he has the **most solves in Rubik's Cube competitions in a year**. This puzzle pro solved 2,033 of 2,122 Rubik's Cubes in World Cube Association competitions—that's the equivalent of more than 5.5 solves every day (and that doesn't include cubes solved outside of official events).

Sébastien also shares the record for the **fewest average moves to complete a Rubik's Cube**, finishing three cubes in an average of 25 moves in 2014. This feat was equaled by **Vincent Shell** in 2014 and **Jan Bentlage** in 2015.

ROBOT RECORD

Human beings aren't the only ones taking on Rubik's Cubes. On March 15, 2014, a robot called **CUBESTORMER 3** (pictured), built by Brits Mike Dobson and David Gilday out of LEGO®, unscrambled a puzzle in 3.25 seconds, becoming the **fastest robot to solve a Rubik's Cube**. However, in 2016, a new robot called **Sub1** took the crown with a lightning-quick 0.887 seconds! The bot was built by Albert Beer of Germany.

UNSOLVABLE?

Dutch scientist **Oskar van Deventer** began designing puzzles at the age of 12. He has since created one that's so complex, no one has been able to solve it! It's the **largest order magic cube**, at 17 by 17 by 17 cubes, and contains 1,539 parts. Oskar presented it at the New York Puzzle Party Symposium on February 12, 2011, and the puzzle-loving crowd went wild! He says that if you can solve a regular Rubik's Cube, you can potentially solve his cube—but it would take a *lot* of work!

LIVING LARGE

The **largest mechanical puzzle** is Quest, a 3D geometrically symmetrical puzzle, which was designed and built by **Joe Pieczynski** in his garage. Just how big is it? The wooden puzzle is 57 inches tall, 52.5 inches in diameter, weighs a whopping 506 pounds, and was unveiled on October 25, 1998, in Austin, Texas. It takes two people around 35 minutes to complete it.

A BIG JIG

Here's a jigsaw puzzle that won't fit in a box. The **largest spherical jigsaw puzzle** measures 15 feet, 7.8 inches in circumference and was made by **Unima Industrial (HK) Ltd.** in Hong Kong, China. The puzzle, which depicts a scene featuring characters from *Winnie the Pooh*, was unveiled at a toy exhibition on January 10, 2005.

A ROYAL RECEPTION

Dave Evans of the UK achieved the Guinness World Records title for the **largest hand-cut jigsaw puzzle** on April 24, 2013. Dave's puzzle is made up of various pictures of Queen Elizabeth's diamond jubilee. Consisting of 40,763 pieces, and measuring 19 feet, 10 inches long and 7 feet, 11 inches high, it took him a little over a month to make. Dave's puzzle received the royal stamp of approval: it was set up at Sandringham, the Queen's country retreat, for six months in 2013!

IF THEY BUILD IT . . .

The 777 people who gathered at the former Kai Tak Airport in Hong Kong, China, on November 3, 2002, weren't there to fly—they were there to build! Together they assembled the world's **largest jigsaw puzzle** by area. Devised by **Great East Asia Surveyors & Consultants Co. Ltd.**, the puzzle measured 58,435.1 square feet and contained 21,600 pieces.

PIECE BY PIECE

Talk about concentration—1,600 students from the **University of Economics** in Ho Chi Minh City in Vietnam gave their full focus on September 24, 2011, when they assembled the **jigsaw puzzle with the most pieces**. These intrepid puzzlers fit together a mind-boggling 551,232 pieces to form a picture that wouldn't even fit in most people's homes, with an overall measurement of 48 feet, 8.64 inches by 76 feet, 1.3 inches. It was so large that they had to complete the jigsaw in a local stadium!

"KNOT" A PROBLEM

A devil's knot is an interlocking puzzle that's a challenge both to put together and to take apart. The **largest devil's knot** was achieved by **Foffa Conrad** of Switzerland on April 16, 2013. Each piece of the puzzle measured 19 feet, 8 inches long by 1 foot, 3 inches wide by 1 foot, 3 inches high.

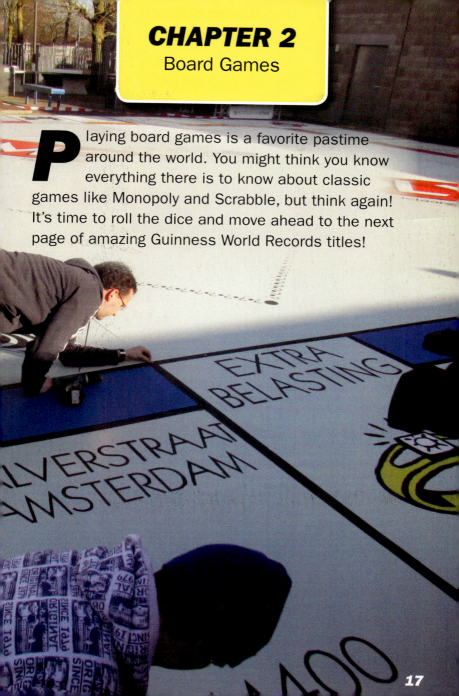

CHAPTER 2
Board Games

Playing board games is a favorite pastime around the world. You might think you know everything there is to know about classic games like Monopoly and Scrabble, but think again! It's time to roll the dice and move ahead to the next page of amazing Guinness World Records titles!

MEGA MONOPOLY

More than 275 million Monopoly games have been sold worldwide, so chances are you might have one at home. However, we're pretty sure you don't have one like this. . . . That's because it's the **largest Monopoly board game**, measuring 4,365.9 square feet. It was created by **Hasbro Poland** in Warsaw, Poland, on September 6, 2015. This also makes it the **largest board game** of any kind! Pass Go and collect . . . a Guinness World Records title!

MONOPOLY GOES GLOBAL

The **most people playing Monopoly simultaneously** was 2,918 people at 21 locations worldwide and online, brought together by **Hasbro** on August 27, 2008.

THE CLASSIC WORD GAME

On March 14, 2006, a total of 1,042 people put their word skills to the test as they took part in 521 games of Scrabble—the **most simultaneous Scrabble games**. The participants, from 65 secondary schools and organizations, came together to set the record at an event arranged by **Northland Secondary School, Mattel Southeast Asia Pte Ltd.**, and **Schools Scrabble Club** in Singapore.

ULTIMATE FACT: One of the most popular board games in the 1980s was Trivial Pursuit, in which players answered questions about geography, entertainment, history, arts and literature, science, and sports. Trivial Pursuit is still played to this day.

RACKING UP WINS

The **most Scrabble opponents played simultaneously** by one challenger is 40 and was achieved by **Lakshan Wanniarachchi** from Sri Lanka on January 4, 2015. Lakshan also jointly holds the record for **highest Scrabble score in 24 hours** with fellow countryman **Yeshan Jayasuriya**. The pair racked up a staggering 196,525 points between them at an event held on November 11–12, 2012.

ULTIMATE FACT:
An unemployed architect named Alfred Mosher Butts invented Scrabble in the 1930s, during the Great Depression, combining anagrams and crossword puzzles into a scoring word game.

ONE BIG GAME

You'd need a big closet to store this game! The world's **biggest board game on sale to the public** is The War Game: World War II, created by **Jeffry Stein** of Burbank, California, and sold by Pegasus Hobbies. The board measures 6 feet, 5.6 inches in length and 3 feet, 2.6 inches in width.

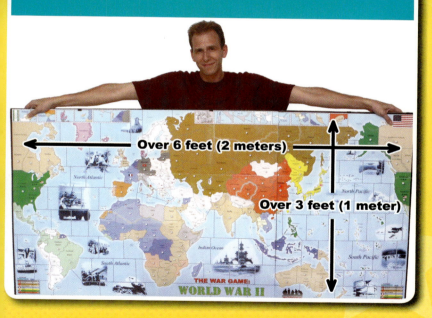

Over 6 feet (2 meters)

Over 3 feet (1 meter)

THE WAR GAME: WORLD WAR II

GAME ON (AND ON AND ON)

Americans **Sam Hennemann** and **Brett Carow** played Strat-O-Matic Baseball for more than two days straight—61 hours, 2 minutes. You couldn't blame them if they forgot whose turn it was! It's the **longest marathon playing a board game** and it took place on June 7–9, 2012, in New York. The pair played the game a total of 116 times during their record-achieving attempt.

FOX GAME

Made by Austrian **Peter Zettel**, the **largest game of Fox and Hen** (aka Fox and Geese) is 19 feet, 8 inches square and was measured in Wildalpen, Austria, on July 9, 2006. You might say Peter's creation "outfoxed" all its rivals!

In this game, one player is the "fox" and tries to catch the birds, while the other player tries to guide the fox into a trap by changing the position of the birds. Peter's game is so huge that kids can take the place of the counters.

REVERSE IT

Reversi is a strategy board game with two players. The board used in Reversi has eight columns and eight rows, and the object is to end up with the most counters still in play by the end. The **largest Reversi board** measures 26 feet, 6 inches by 26 feet, 7 inches, with counters that are 2 feet, 7 inches in diameter. Created by students from **Takada High School** in Japan, it was measured in Tsu, Mie Prefecture, on September 15, 2011.

ROLL THE DICE

Ludo is a popular board game in which two to four players race their game pieces from start to finish according to the roll of the dice. The **largest Ludo board game** measured 31 feet, 7 inches square. It was created by **Adesoye College, Offa**, a coed college in Nigeria, and was presented and measured on July 3, 2012.

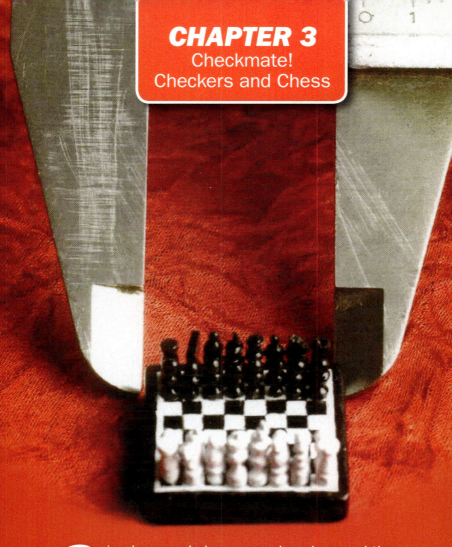

Checkers and chess are played around the world, but only a few select players have earned the recognition of a world record. Whether on land or underwater, at a tournament or in consecutive games, the record holders in this chapter are all masters of the black-and-white board.

CHECKMATE, CEBU!

On January 22, 2012, the **largest board game tournament** took place in Cebu, Philippines. Organized by the **Cebu City Sports Commission**, 43,157 participants pushed their brain power to the limits while playing chess that day.

SERIOUS CONCENTRATION

The **most simultaneous games of international checkers played** is 251 and was conducted by **Jos Stokkel** of the Netherlands on November 6–7, 2010.

International checkers is a variant in which the board is 10 by 10 squares (rather than 8 by 8) and each participant starts with 20 counters (instead of 12).

CHECKERS FOR EVERYONE

The **most people playing checkers at once** is 540 and was achieved at an event organized by the **PHP Agency LLC** in Nevada on February 8, 2014.

A CHECKERED COAT

The coat of arms of Trebbin, Germany, features a checkerboard, so on June 14, 2013—to commemorate the 800th anniversary of the city—**Stadt Trebbin** staged the **largest checkers tournament**, consisting of 574 people. In the final showdown, Clemens Crucius defeated Detlev Kuhnen to take first place and win the contest.

BLOWING BUBBLES

Ordinary checkers just isn't extreme enough for some people, so **Normunds Pakulis** of Latvia thought: Why not throw some scuba diving gear into the mix? The **most people playing checkers underwater** was 88 at a gymnasium in Riga, Latvia, on May 21, 2011. The boards were fixed to the bottom of a pool for the aquatic contest and the checkers didn't float away because they were made of lead!

CHESS-HEAD

Anna-Maria Botsari of Greece has played a lot of chess in her life, but never as many games in a row as she did on February 27–28, 2001. Over the two days, she achieved the record for **most consecutive chess games**, an incredible 1,102. Staggeringly, she won all the games except for seven draws.

INFINITY CHESS

The **most simultaneous games of chess played against different opponents** is 523. It was achieved by Grand Master **Alik Gershon** of Israel at an event organized by the Israeli Chess Federation, at Rabin Square in Tel Aviv, Israel, on October 21–22, 2010. Alik won 454 of the games, lost 11, and drew 58.

MAGNIFYING GLASS NEEDED

The **smallest handmade chess set** was created by Indian railway employee **Malla Siva**. Made out of slate with a series of fine needles and other custom tools, this teeny-tiny board measures just 0.7 inches square; the largest piece is 0.26 inches tall and the smallest is 0.16 inches. It was measured in Bilaspur, India, on March 3, 2008.

BODACIOUS BOARD

The **largest chess set**, on the other hand, measures 19 feet, 4 inches on each side. The king is 47 inches tall and spans 1 foot, 2 inches wide at the base. The set comprises a painted concrete board and teakwood pieces and was made by the **Medicine Hat Chess Club** in Alberta, Canada, in 2009.

KINGPIN

The **largest chess piece** measures 16 feet, 7 inches tall with a 6-foot, 8-inch diameter at its base. This giant king was created by **Gitok Secondary School** in Belgium in order to raise money and awareness for charities and was measured on April 4, 2014.

HE'S ALL SET

The **largest collection of chess sets** is 412, as of 2012, and belongs to **Akın Gökyay** of Ankara, Turkey. Having started his collection back in 1975, Akın hopes to one day open a dedicated museum to display his pride and joy.

GAME ON

The **most games of chess played simultaneously** was 20,480 and was achieved by the **Sports Authority of Gujarat** in India, at the University of Gujarat Sports Grounds, Ahmedabad, on December 24, 2010. The tournament consisted of 1,024 chess masters competing against more than 20,000 amateurs.

YOUR (GURGLE) MOVE

Hold your breath for this record: it's the **longest time playing chess underwater**! Wearing diving gear, Swedish divers **Olle Widell** and **Edvin Bengtsson** played the game of strategy in a tank of water on June 3–4, 2013, for 25 hours, 14 minutes.

CHAPTER 4
Wheels and Wings

Whether taking flight or leaving dust in their tracks, the owners of the model vehicles in this chapter know that being the longest, smallest, lightest, fastest, and largest are surefire ways to earn a hallowed spot in the record books! So put on your seat belt and get ready for a record-setting ride!

LOOPIN' IT UP

You might say that this record runs circles around the rest of the competition! The **largest loop-the-loop with a remote-controlled (RC) model vehicle** is 10 feet, 5 inches and was achieved by the British television program *The Gadget Show* in Birmingham, UK, on June 15, 2013. The feat was performed on a Venom VMX-450 RC dirt bike, driven by presenter **Jason Bradbury** of the UK.

JUMP TO IT

Vrooom! Vrooom! Leaping into the record books is the **longest ramp jump by an RC car**, clearing a gap of 121 feet, 0.75 inches. The jump was achieved by a Carson Specter 6S and at the controls was **Thomas Strobel** of Germany at an event called SPEEDWEEKS held in Sonneberg, Germany, on July 30, 2011.

DOWN UNDER DISTANCE

The **greatest distance covered by a battery-powered RC car on a single charge** is 23.79 miles. The 1:10-scale Formula 1 car was driven by **David Stevens** of Australia at the Templestowe Flat Track Racing Club in Victoria, Australia, on April 20, 2013.

TAKING FLIGHT

The **Radio Controlled Helicopter Association** rallied 98 members and their toy choppers on September 8, 2013, to achieve the **most remote-controlled (RC) helicopters airborne simultaneously.** On the same day, the group also set the record for **most inverted RC helicopters airborne simultaneously,** with 53 hovering upside down at once.

LIGHT FLIGHT

It's not as light as a feather, but it's pretty close: the **lightest RC model helicopter** is the **PicooZ MX-1** made by Silverlit Toys Manufactory of Hong Kong, China. It weighs a mere 0.28 ounces and the remote transmitter is also the helicopter's "hangar" where the toy recharges.

SOARING HIGH

Is it a bird? Is it a plane? Kind of. It's the **fastest RC jet-powered model aircraft**! The turbine-powered airplane, created by **Niels Herbrich** of Germany, reached a top speed of 439.29 miles per hour—about 80% of the cruising speed of a Boeing 777—at the WLP Ballenstedt airfield in Saxony-Anhalt, Germany, sending it soaring into the record books on September 14, 2013.

Dominoes aren't just for playing at your kitchen table. The people behind these top toy achievements have toppled them underwater, built a gigantic wall with them, and gathered by the thousands to play with them! You'll also read about a few records inspired by dominoes, which have taken toppling to a whole other level.

DA BOMB

After painstakingly lining up 54,321 dominoes at the Wilhelm-Lückert-Gymnasium in Büdingen, Germany, on August 16, 2014, what did the stackers do? Push them down again! But all the hard work was worth it, as **Sinners Domino Entertainment** of Germany picked up the Guinness World Records title for **most dominoes toppled in a circle bomb**!

ULTIMATE FACT:
The earliest dominoes evolved from dice games, with the tiles representing all possible outcomes from a roll of two dice.

NOW THAT'S ALL WET!

Did you ever wonder if you could stack dominoes underwater? Well, wonder no more! **Sinners Domino Entertainment** also achieved the **most dominoes toppled underwater by a team** on August 16, 2014, with 10,489 dominoes toppled in a shallow pool at the Wilhelm-Lückert-Gymnasium (above).

Four days earlier, on August 12, they claimed the title for **most dominoes stacked on a single piece**—1,055! The free-standing tower stayed upright for nearly one and a half hours.

IT TAKES TWO

Americans **Brittany Bova** and **Markey Munive** were all business on May 23, 2015. That was the day the duo set a new record for **fastest time to stack a set of dominoes**. They completed the task in an incredible 20.78 seconds at the Guinness World Records Museum in Hollywood, California.

STACKING THEM UP

Multi-record-breaker **Silvio Sabba** of Italy did what he does best on April 28, 2013, by adding another Guinness World Records title to his collection! He piled up 48 dominoes in a half minute, the **most dominoes stacked in 30 seconds**, in Pioltello, Milan, Italy. This beat his own previous personal best by . . . one domino! He also holds the record for **most dominoes stacked in 30 seconds using chopsticks**: 40 dominoes.

DOMINOES DOWN

On May 10, 2013, Japan's **Team Shuzo** achieved the **most dominoes toppled in one minute by eight people**. At a Sinfonia Technology Co., Ltd. team-building event, held in Ise, Mie, Japan, 260 dominoes were knocked down. You might say they fell like . . . dominoes.

WONDER WALL

The **longest domino wall** stretched a staggering 98 feet, 5 inches long and consisted of 31,405 dominoes. It was erected and toppled by the pro domino society **Sinners Domino Entertainment** at the Wilhelm-Lückert-Gymnasium in Büdingen, Germany, on July 6, 2012.

DOMINO DOMINATION

The **most people playing dominoes** simultaneously is 3,344 at an event organized by **Luis Alberto Ramirez Feliz** of the Dominican Republic. The domino jamboree was held in the Caribbean island's capital city, Santo Domingo, on January 22, 2012.

TAKE THE PLUNGE

The **Del Mar Dive Club** sure knows how to make a splash. They achieved the **most people playing dominoes underwater**, getting 60 players to don their swimwear at the diving center in Wigston, Leicestershire, UK, on August 27, 2013. The attempt consisted of 15 games of dominoes, each being played by four divers.

DISC DOMINOES

Taking three days to set up, the **most disc cases toppled like dominoes** is 5,969, achieved by German **Tim Weißker**, at Dientzenhofer-Gymnasium in Bamberg, Germany, on September 12, 2011. This bettered his previous record by 969 cases!

STACKING BOOKS

The **Sinners Domino Entertainment** team struck once again at the Frankfurt Book Fair on October 14, 2015. The dedicated domino masters successfully set up and knocked over 10,200 copies of *Guinness World Records 2016* to take the record for **most books toppled in a domino fashion**.

ULTIMATE FACT: A standard "double-six" domino set consists of 28 tiles, but much rarer "double-21" sets have a staggering 253 tiles!

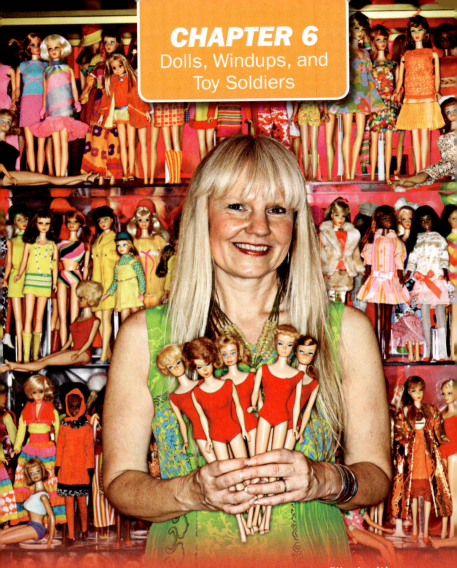

CHAPTER 6
Dolls, Windups, and Toy Soldiers

Can you imagine an entire house filled with Barbies? Or a display of over 68,000 PLAYMOBIL figurines? Well, you can see them for yourself as we enter a new chapter of records focused on beloved playthings—and a seriously massive stuffed toy snake!

ALL DOLLED UP

Children around the world love to line up their dolls, but **VOLKS Inc.** took this tradition to a whole new level with the **longest line of dolls**. A total of 3,282 dolls, called "Dollfies," were lined up at Tokyo Big Sight in Japan, on December 22, 2013. Each had a unique hairstyle and clothing, and their height varied from 10.6 inches to some in excess of two feet tall.

QUEEN OF THE BARBIES

Bettina Dorfmann of Germany began collecting Barbies in 1993, and hers is now the **largest collection of Barbie dolls** in the world. As of October 2011, Bettina had over 15,000 Barbies, filling up every spare corner of her home. She says she began collecting the dolls because she loved them as a child—though the first doll she received was actually Midge, Barbie's best friend. Many of Bettina's dolls are on exhibit around the world, and this avid collector has vowed to never stop adding new members to her Barbie family.

ULTIMATE FACT:

Barbie was created by American Ruth Handler, inspired by watching her daughter, Barbara, play with paper dolls. Barbie made her debut on March 9, 1959, at the American International Toy Fair in New York, and that day is Barbie's official birthday.

STITCH BY STITCH

Imagine how much work goes into making just one of these felt dolls. Well, **Isabel Romero Jorques** of Spain has made 500 of them, making hers the **largest collection of handmade dolls**. Isabel proved you don't need fancy kits to make a doll. With only a needle, a pair of scissors, and a thimble, she made all of the 3.9-inch-tall dolls in just three months. Each one is unique, with different dresses, hair, and facial features.

MINI ME

Russian nesting dolls, also known as *matryoshka*, are hollow wooden dolls that are placed inside each other from smallest to largest. The **largest set of Russian nesting dolls** is a 51-piece set hand-painted by **Youlia Bereznitskaia** of Russia. When they were completed in 2003, the largest doll measured 1 foot, 9.25 inches tall, and the smallest was a mere 0.125 inches. Traditionally, the dolls would be decorated with a theme, such as Russian fairy tales, but today nesting dolls can depict everything from athletes and politicians to celebrities.

PAPER PALS

On July 7, 2013, **Amna Al Fard** of the United Arab Emirates assembled 1,145 paper dolls at the Maraya Art Centre, UAE, to achieve the **largest display of handmade**

paper dolls. Amna has won several awards for her paper quilling—the technique she uses to make her dolls—and is a member of the American Quilling Guild. Amna said: "Everything is possible in a world made out of paper. I am able to create a world that I read about in children's books [and] make it real with thin paper strips."

YOU'RE WINDING ME UP . . .

The **largest collection of windup toys** contains 1,042 items, as of November 26, 2011, and belongs to **William Keuntje** of Landing, New Jersey. What started off as a Christmas present in 1975 mushroomed into a massive collection, thanks in large part to donations and gifts from William's friends and family. To celebrate his world record attempt, William hosted an event at his home featuring a quiz about his favorite toys. The prize for the winner? You guessed it . . . a windup toy!

GOOD SOLDIERS

Jonathan Perry Waters from Macon, Georgia, marched straight into the record books. This toy soldier enthusiast had 1,080 figurines as of February 28, 2016—the **largest collection of toy soldiers** in the world. He's been building up his massive toy army since he was just five years old.

PLAYTIME!

The **largest PLAYMOBIL display** consisted of 68,808 figurines and was achieved by **Aesclick** (Association of Spanish Collectibles of PLAYMOBIL) in Barbastro, Spain, on September 26, 2010.

Approximately 2.7 billion of the play figures have been produced since the first toys were created in 1974 by German craftsman Hans Beck. If they could all hold hands, the figures would circle the world nearly three and a half times!

ULTIMATE FACT:
Each PLAYMOBIL figure has seven parts: hair, head, torso, two arms, one set of legs, and an inner mechanism.

TEAMING FOR TOYS

Gunma Tsurushi-Kazari no Kai of Japan put on quite a show on December 27, 2014, with the **largest display of handmade stuffed toys**. Presented in a 24-foot-plus-tall walk-through display, 13,556 silk figures of Japanese animals and historical articles were tied through strings and hung up in Gunma Prefecture. More than 1,200 people of all ages helped to make the toys for over a year, determined to take back the record from the neighboring Niigata Prefecture.

SNAKE, RATTLE, AND ROLL

The **longest stuffed toy snake** measured a mind-boggling 5,803 feet, 1.66 inches—that's over a mile! It was made by **Hastings Community House** in Victoria, Australia, and was verified on March 22, 2013. The project was a wonderful group effort, involving many local senior citizens and other members of the community who knitted and crafted the superlative serpent. It took them over 20 months to make *hisssssssstory!*

Certain toys have earned their place in history as classics. Chances are you've either played with them yourself or perhaps you've seen them in your attic or at a garage sale! The iconic toys in this chapter set the standard for having fun, challenging kids' creativity, and inspiring imaginations.

MAGIC *Etch A Sketch* SCREEN

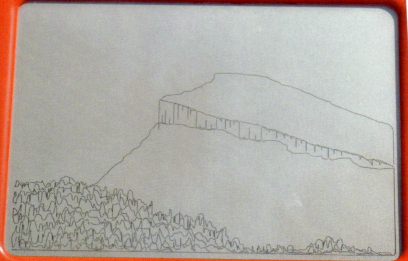

SHAKE

THIS ETCH-A-SK
WAS USED TO S
OFFICIAL GUIN
WORLD REC

"WORLDS LAF
MASS OF PE
ETCH-A-SKET

JUNE 25, 2
LYONS, COLC
USA

SKETCHAPALO

THE DRAW OF THE ETCH A SKETCH

One of the most recognizable American toys is the Ohio Art Company's Etch A Sketch. The first one rolled off the assembly line in the summer of 1960 and, 60 years later, the toy is still going strong. The **most people drawing on an Etch A Sketch at once** is 372 and was achieved at an event organized by **Jeff Gagliardi** and **Clark Hodge** in Lyons, Colorado, on June 25, 2011.

DON'T FALL!

In the classic body-bending game Twister, players have to put their hands and feet on different colored spots without falling over. But on the **largest Twister board** the game is taken to a much grander scale. Combining 1,200 standard Twister boards, the massive mat spanned 171 feet, 3 inches by 158 feet, 5.5 inches. It was created by country music star **Thomas Rhett** and **Big Machine Label Group** at the AT&T Stadium in Arlington, Texas, on September 23, 2015, as part of a week-long event called "Tangled Up in Texas."

NO YO-KE

The **largest simultaneous yo-yo** was achieved by 2,036 participants at an event organized by **Yomega Corporation** and *Boys' Life Magazine* at the 2010 National Scout Jamboree in Fort A.P. Hill, Virginia. This smashed the previous record by 1,479 yo-yoers.

ULTIMATE FACT: Have you ever "walked the dog" with a yo-yo? This is a trick in which you release the yo-yo, let it spin, then allow it to roll across the floor before tugging it back to your hand.

A DIZZYING DISPLAY

American **John "Lucky" Meisenheimer** first fell in love with yo-yos when he was in junior high in the early 1970s. When he grew up and went to medical school, he began playing with yo-yos as a way to help him relax between classes. Lucky's collection grew to 4,586, the **largest collection of yo-yos** as of February 22, 2010. He's an author, too, self-publishing *Lucky's Collectors' Guide to 20th-Century Yo-Yos.*

STRINGING ALONG

Now this is a yo-yo you can't fit in the palm of your hand! Taking three years to construct, the **largest yo-yo** is 11 feet, 9 inches in diameter and weighs in at 4,620 pounds. It was devised by American **Beth Johnson** in La Rue, Ohio, and verified on September 15, 2012. It was a nail-biting photo shoot as it was quite windy when Beth climbed on top of the mega-toy to have her picture taken.

CORNY CONTEST

Cornhole is a popular game in which players take turns throwing bags of corn at a board with a hole in the far end. The **largest game of cornhole** measured 64 feet, 3 inches long and 32 feet, 2 inches wide, with an 8-foot diameter hole. It was created by the **Goodyear Tire & Rubber Company** in Pompano Beach, Florida, on December 28, 2015.

PINBALL WHIZ

A few quarters last a long time at the arcade for **Alessandro Parisi** of Australia. He holds the record title for the **longest pinball marathon**, lasting 28 hours at the Westland Shopping Centre in Whyalla, Australia, on January 22–23, 2007.

PINBALL FOR GIANTS

The **largest pinball machine**, meanwhile, measures 53 feet, 9 inches long by 24 feet, 7 inches wide, and was made by **Heineken Italia**. Demonstrated during Milan Design Week in Italy on April 12, 2014, the installation turned a normal living room, including sofas, tables, and a bar, into a supersize pinball table!

POGO POP

Hopping his way into the record books and "bursting" the competition's bubble is **Mark Aldridge** of the UK. He achieved the **most balloons popped using a pogo stick** on the set of *Lo Show dei Record* in Italy, taking out 57 balloons in just a minute on April 1, 2010.

ULTIMATE FACT:
The pogo stick was invented and patented in 1918 by George Hansburg. He formed Flybar, Inc., the largest pogo stick manufacturer in the world, which to date has sold over 25 million pogo sticks!

JUST DUCKY

When **Charlotte Lee** takes a bath, she's never at a loss for tub toys. As of April 10, 2011, this American collector owned the **largest collection of rubber ducks**—a quacktastic 5,631! She began collecting the squeaky toys in 1996, and displays them all inside glass cases in her dedicated "duck room." The ducks come in all shapes and sizes; some glow, some have special scents (like strawberries!), and some are even big enough to sit on.

ROUND AND ROUND

The **longest distance swinging on rings while Hula-Hooping** is 272 feet. Super-strong **Jeffrey Clark Nash** of the USA swung into the record books after achieving this feat on April 11, 2013, in Santa Monica, California.

The **most Hula-Hoops spun at once** is 200, achieved by Australian hooping instructor **Marawa Ibrahim** in Los Angeles, California, on November 25, 2015. It is the fourth time that "Marawa the Amazing" has broken this record, with her latest success bettering her first by 40 hoops!

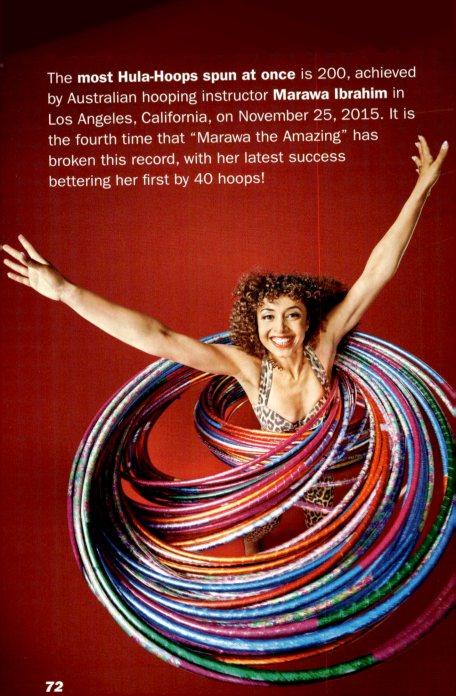

CHAPTER 8
Super-Toys!

Is the whoopee cushion the best toy ever? Judging by all the smiles it raises, it just might be! But there are a few more contenders in this chapter. From model trains and giant crayons to bobbleheads, this next dip into the Guinness World Records toy box is guaranteed to entertain and amuse.

WHAT A GAS

If you ever want to play a prank on a giant, this is what you need. . . . Made by New Zealand kids' TV show *What Now*, the **largest whoopee cushion** spanned 19 feet, 9.48 inches when it was measured before being inflated on September 28, 2014. Once it was filled with air, it required 15 people pushing down on it to produce its trademark noise!

CAR-TISTIC LICENSE

The **largest toy car mosaic** measured 115.89 square feet and was created by **Mini China** in Guangzhou, China, on June 15, 2013. A total of 1,034 toy cars were used for the artwork, which depicted the Union Jack, the national flag of the UK.

PASS ON THE LEFT

The **longest line of toy cars** consisted of 24,189 vehicles and was created by the **National Motor Museum** in Beaulieu, UK, on May 5, 2014. You might say it was quite a traffic jam . . . the line measured around 1.2 miles.

CHOO-CHOO CHAMPIONS!

Stretching 8,553 feet, 7 inches long, the **longest wooden toy-train track** was constructed at a festival with the guidance of Swedish toy company **Brio AB** and **Siemens AG Rail System Division** of Germany in 2012. Assembled by parents and children attending the festival in Wegberg, Germany, the final structure comprised 1,990 curved pieces and 10,371 straight lengths of track.

ALL ABOARD!

Created by twin brothers **Frederik** and **Gerrit Braun** of Germany, the **largest model railway** has a total track length of 39,370 feet and covers an area of 14,000 square feet, and resides at the Minatur Wunderland attraction in Hamburg, Germany. Re-creating areas of Europe and the USA, the landscape includes many famous cities and landmarks, including Las Vegas, the Grand Canyon, and Mount Rushmore, as well as being home to 200,000 figurines!

LITTLE FUN

Have you heard of MicroPets? Launched by Japanese toymaker **TOMY**, the original series of the **smallest sound-activated, self-powered toy** came in a range of 10 different characters and measured no more than 1.37 inches tall, easily fitting in the palm of the hand. The MicroPets could talk, play, or sing, and were first shown at the Tokyo Toy Fair in Japan in May 2002.

COLOR IN THE LINES

The **largest crayon** weighed 731 pounds, stood 9 feet, 9 inches tall, and was created by American **Benjamin Chase Carey** and **Petey's Promise** in Concord, North Carolina, on October 29, 2011. The waxy wonder was made by melting down thousands of regular-size crayons and pouring the liquid into a giant mold. Wonder if there's a crayon box big enough to hold it . . .

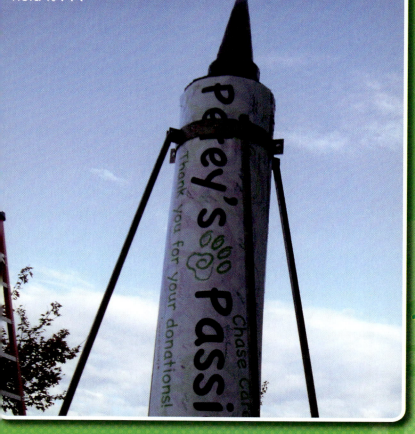

SKYSCRAPER

K'NEX® Manufacturing built the **tallest K'NEX tower** in Bedford, UK, on June 5–6, 1999— a structure measuring 101 feet, 3.6 inches tall. The tower was built on a 6-foot, 6.7-inch square base and contained 50,342 pieces.

SUPERSONIC K'NEX-ION

The **largest K'NEX sculpture**, meanwhile, is 12 feet, 8.3 inches high by 8 feet wide by 43 feet, 10.7 inches long, and was achieved by the **BLOODHOUND SSC RBLI K'NEX Build Team** of the UK on August 26, 2014. Using in excess of 350,000 K'NEX pieces, the sculpture was an actual-size model of the Bloodhound supercar, which is aiming to surpass 1,000 miles per hour to set a new land-speed record.

A NOD TO A GAME GREAT

The **Game Show Network** not only broadcasts exciting television shows; they also created some Guinness World Records excitement with the world's **largest bobblehead**! Standing 11 feet tall, the giant bobblehead was a likeness of legendary game show host Chuck Woolery (the original host of *Wheel of Fortune*). The final figure weighed 900 pounds and was displayed at the McCormick Place convention center in Chicago, Illinois, on June 8, 2003.

ULTIMATE FACT:
A bobblehead is connected to its body by a hook, so that when you tap the head, it will wobble, bobble, and nod!

Letting your imagination run free is one of the best parts of playing with building blocks. Here you'll find some amazing construction records, each achieved one block at a time

LEGO

CLONE ZONE

The Force was with **LEGO® UK** on June 27, 2008. On that day, they assembled the **largest display of Star Wars Clone Troopers**, which were all LEGO Minifigures. The out-of-this-galaxy display in Slough, UK, was composed of 35,210 individual models!

LIFE-SIZE LEGO

TV host **James May** of the UK rounded up 1,200
volunteers to help build the **largest life-size LEGO house**
in Dorking, UK, on September 17, 2009, for the TV series
Toy Stories. Comprising 2.4 million bricks, the house
was 15 feet, 4 inches high, 30 feet, 9 inches long,
and 18 feet, 10 inches wide. It had two floors and
four rooms, which even included some furnishings and
appliances, such as a toaster and an iron (inset).

LEGO LEGEND

US Marine **Kyle Ugone**, a resident of Yuma, Arizona, boasts the **largest collection of complete LEGO sets**. He acquired his first sets in 1986, and as of July 23, 2011, he owned 1,091.

NO LEANING TOWER

The regularly contested **tallest LEGO structure** was completed by **LEGO Italia**, soaring into the record books on June 21, 2015. It measured 114 feet, 11 inches, and used an estimated 550,000 LEGO bricks, assembled by some 18,000 builders over a period of four days.

BRICK PICK

At a dedicated LEGO event held in London, UK, in November 2014, Brit **Megane Scott** speedily stacked 37 bricks, achieving the **most LEGO bricks picked up with one brick in 30 seconds**. A day later, **Nardy Nafzger** from the Netherlands matched Megane's feat, so the pair (pictured below) currently share the record.

LEGO-REX

Ever wondered what would happen if you crossed Jurassic Park with LEGO? At 20 feet long and made up of 80,020 pieces, *Dinosaur Skeleton* was built by American artist **Nathan Sawaya** during the summer of 2011. The true-to-life-size model of a *Tyrannosaurus rex* is the **largest complete LEGO skeleton** and is one of the star exhibits on his traveling show, *The Art of the Brick*.

CHAPTER 10
Video Games

Being an ultimate gamer has its rewards, as you'll learn after reading about the achievements of these Guinness World Records title holders. Whether it's a treasure trove of Pokémon goodies, the biggest arcade machine in the world, or the team who had an incredible payday, gaming offers everyone the chance to level up and earn a record.

READY PLAYER ONE

Gamers don't come much more dedicated than **Michael Thomasson** of Hamburg, New York, who amassed the **largest collection of video games** in the world: 10,607 games as counted on December 3, 2012.

This übercollector received his first game, *Cosmic Avenger*, on Christmas Eve at the age of 12, but he had to wait a whole year to get a ColecoVision console to play it on. Believe it or not, he sold his first game collection when he went to college in 1988, but when the Sega Genesis was released the next year, he began to rebuild his collection. Happily, he hung on to the ColecoVision, and has said it's one of his favorite items.

It took Michael decades to acquire his collection, but he says, he "spent very little money doing it," suggesting that bartering is the secret to keeping costs down. He didn't have the opportunity to play every game, as a lot of his time is taken up designing his own video games as well as teaching around the subject.

In 2015, the collection was sold to "a well-known celebrity" who wishes to remain anonymous.

GAME CHANGER

Jason Camberis of the USA created the world's **largest arcade machine**. This giant cabinet measures 14 feet, 5.6 inches tall—about the same height as a double-decker bus—3 feet, 5.7 inches deep, and 6 feet, 3.9 inches wide. It was unveiled in Bensenville, Illinois, on March 23, 2015. Among other games, it features the classic arcade title *PAC-MAN*.

MICRO GAMING!

Mark Slevinsky of Canada knows that good things come in small packages. The computer engineer built the **smallest arcade machine**. The diminutive cabinet measures just 4.88 by 2.05 by 2.36 inches and is fully playable. Mark made it from scratch in 2009 and he even wrote his own operating system, FunkOS, to program its *Tetris*, *Space Invaders*, and *Breakout* clones.

NINTENDO'S BIGGEST FAN

The **largest collection of Nintendo memorabilia** belongs to police officer **Ahmed Bin Fahad** from the United Arab Emirates. His collection consists of 2,020 items, and was verified on November 12, 2014.

One of the rarest items in his collection is an M8 Demo Unit from one of Nintendo's original 1980s kiosks. Ahmed is particularly proud of the fact that he has every edition of *Super Mario Bros.* and the *Legend of Zelda* games.

PEDAL TO THE MEDAL

Leyla Hasso of the UK is a speed demon when it comes to *Super Mario Kart*. She achieved the **fastest Super Mario Kart time trial by a female gamer** on the PAL version of Vanilla Lake 2 when she was 14 years, 9 months old. How fast was she? She clocked a blistering 51.87 seconds at the Games Expo East Kent, in Margate, UK, on February 22, 2014.

SPEEDY SAMI

The **fastest completion of Mario Circuit 1 in *Super Mario Kart* PAL edition** was set by **Sami Çetin** of the UK. He completed the track in 57.9 seconds on December 25, 2013. Sami also holds the same record for the **NTSC version** of the game; an even quicker 55.97 seconds on November 23, 2014.

MINECRAFT MARATHON

On August 19–20, 2011, **Paul Dahloff** of Germany, along with Austrians **Hanns Peter Glock**, **Stefan Reichspfarrer**, and **Martin Fornleitner** (pictured), achieved the **longest marathon on a cell phone game**. The four block-loving gamers used a Sony Xperia handset to play *Minecraft* for 24 hours, 10 minutes in Vienna, Austria.

PAYDAY PAYOUT

Sometimes gaming can earn you big bucks, as proved by **Team NewBee** of China (pictured) in July 2014. The competitive eSports team won the **largest payout for a team in any video-gaming tournament:** a cool $5,028,121 at the fourth annual international *Dota 2* championship competition, the International 4, held in Seattle, Washington. Incredibly, Team NewBee has since lost their record at the 2015 edition of the same event; US gamers **Evil Geniuses** took home a total prize of $6,634,661!

IT PAYS TO PLAY

US gamer **Katherine Gunn**, aka "Mystik", also knows a thing or two about turning a profit out of video games. Since 2007, she has accumulated $122,000 from tournaments playing titles such as *Dead or Alive* and *Halo*, making her the **highest earning female gamer** in the world.

OUI, WII

The **most consecutive one-game wins of *Wii Sports Tennis* against multiple players** is 21, and was set by **Staš Kostrzewski** of France at the Virgin Megastore in Paris on November 7, 2007, as part of the Guinness World Records Day celebrations.

STRIKE!

Lots of things are big in Texas so perhaps it's no surprise that the **largest *Wii Sports Bowling* tournament** took place there! Organized by **TexanPlus** and held at the Reliant Center in Houston, on October 1, 2009, it featured 436 participants, all of whom were senior citizens. Proving that video games are for all ages, the tournament was part of a health fair at which the seniors were offered advice and free vaccinations.

GOTTA CATCH 'EM ALL!

Lisa Courtney of the UK has been collecting Pokémon since she was nine years old and can now lay claim to the **largest collection of Pokémon memorabilia**, with 14,410 different items as of October 14, 2010. Lisa's incredible collection includes items from the UK, USA, France, and, of course, Japan. She has made several trips to Japan to collect Pokémon merchandise, each time shipping boxes back home!

Games play an important role in every culture around the world—and every single one has the potential to be given a Guinness World Records twist. From exchanging secret gifts to picking up sticks, and en-masse dancing, this chapter is all about superlative recreation. Who says playtime can't also be record time?

KEEP DANCING

The **most people participating in a dance video game** is 10,730, boogying to "DJ Got Us Fallin' in Love Again" by Usher. The epic dance-off was organized by **Starfloor** and was led by a choreographer at Palais Omnisports de Paris-Bercy in Paris, France, on November 26, 2011.

FREEZE-FRAME

Hold that pose! The **largest game of musical statues** was achieved by 1,079 participants at an event organized by **Danone Finland** at the Helsinki Exhibition Center in Finland on April 25, 2010. Musical statues is similar to musical chairs: players dance to music and when the music stops, everyone has to freeze. If you keep moving or don't stop fast enough, you're kicked off the dance floor!

CHRISTMAS CHEER

On December 4, 2013, the students in Lexington, Kentucky, had a serious case of holiday spirit! Feeling festive, 1,463 pupils (pictured) from **Lexington Catholic High School** and local middle schools participated in the **largest Secret Santa game in a single location**, achieving the record while spreading joy. Meanwhile, the **largest Secret Santa game in multiple locations** was attended by 4,557 people in the Philippines, Hong Kong, Taiwan, and Singapore, as part of an event organized by **Globe Telecom, Inc.** (Philippines) on December 18, 2011.

RINGS AROUND THE COMPETITION

Demonstrating a Frodo Baggins–like determination to destroy the One Ring, **William Stone**, **Bryan Erwin**, and **Christopher Groetzinger** took part in the **longest trading card marathon** from December 27, 2002, to January 1, 2003. The trio played a total 154 rounds of the *Lord of the Rings* Trading Card Game over a period of 128 hours to earn themselves a very "precious" record.

GATHER 'EM UP!

The **largest game of pick-up sticks** could have been called "pick-up poles"! It consisted of 30 supersize "sticks"—seven yellow, seven red, seven blue, eight green, and one black—each measuring 29 feet, 10.3 inches long. Four teams of 112 children took to the playing fields of **St. John's Preparatory School** in Harare, Zimbabwe, to get involved with this scaled-up version of the classic game on July 21, 2007.

CHESS WITH A TWIST

The **most games of shogi played simultaneously** is 1,574 at Tokyo Big Sight, an event arranged by the **Japan Shogi Association**, **Japan Tobacco Inc.**, and **TableMark Co. Ltd.**, on November 18, 2012. The two-player strategy board game is considered by some as a Japanese version of chess but players can keep captured pieces and then use them as their own.

GO FISH

The world's **largest game of kingyosukui** involved a tank that was 330 feet, 8.5 inches long, containing 60,000 goldfish, 15,000 *medaka* (Japanese killifish), and 2,199 gallons of water. Kingyosukui is a traditional Japanese game, often played at summer festivals, in which players gather fish using a special scooper. The record game was held in Kanagawa, Japan, on August 4, 2002, and was organized by **Masaaki Tanaka** from the Guild of Fujisawa Ginza Doyokai.

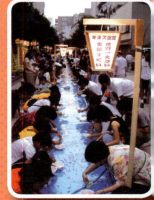

CHAPTER 12
Paws for Thought

Originally named after President Theodore Roosevelt, teddy bears have been some of our best-loved toys since the early 20th century, often staying with their owners for a lifetime. So what better way to close this book than by shining a spotlight on some record-breaking teddies?

TRAVELING TEDDY

If this little toy bear named **Raymondo** could talk, he'd have some amazing stories to tell. He's the **most traveled toy mascot**, covering 395,605 miles from September 27, 2009, to September 3, 2010, and passing through six continents and 35 countries on his journey!

Representing Inflight Sales Person of the Year (ISPY), Raymondo accompanied airline crew members or sponsors on his adventure. He traveled with a suitcase of supplies, his "passport," and several changes of clothing. Each mile was logged on a dedicated website, along with a personal blog and pictures. After visiting Aruba, Australia, Bahrain, Canada, China, Cuba, Cyprus, Egypt, Finland, France, Germany, Greece, Hong Kong, India, Indonesia, Iran, Ireland, Italy, Jordan, Lebanon, Malaysia, Mexico, Singapore, South Africa, South Korea, Spain, Sudan, Syria, Taiwan, Thailand, Turkey, United Arab Emirates, the United Kingdom, the USA, and Vietnam, Raymondo was more than ready for retirement.

ULTIMATE FACT:
Raymondo was named after Ray Martin, the husband of ISPY founder Christine Martin.

BEARY GOOD

Don't cut the line—unless you're a teddy bear! On May 3, 2015, **Finlay Church** of the UK achieved the **longest line of teddy bears**. A total of 15,534 teddies formed an orderly line at the Alvechurch Cricket Club in Worcestershire, UK.

TINY TEDS

Cheryl Moss of South Africa knows that no matter how small, a teddy bear can be a forever friend. She's been making "microbears" for over six years. The **smallest stitched teddy bears on sale to the public** average about 0.43 inches long—smaller than a dime!